TRIATHLON
THE ESSENTIAL
TRAINING LOG

CAROLINE & JUSTIN HATTEE

1st Edition: 2019.

Design by Matt Tarrant.

The thoughts and ideas expressed throughout this book (and related publications) have developed through years of research, training, racing and coaching kids. We've clearly benefited from a huge amount of practise, trial and error, and through gaining British Triathlon coaching certification.

Instagram @strive4tri

-

For all the Ketton Panthers

ALSO BY CAROLINE & JUSTIN HATTEE

KIDS' TRIATHLON: THE ESSENTIAL GUIDE

Foreword by Vicky Holland
(Olympic Bronze Medalist and ITU World Champion)

Available from Amazon

THIS BOOK
BELONGS TO:

NAME

ADDRESS

EMAIL

EMERGENCY CONTACT

DATE FROM

DATE TO

CLUB/S

AGE CATEGORY

COUNTRY

REGION

**NATIONAL FEDERATION
MEMBERSHIP NUMBER**

CONTENTS

PREFACE

Whilst this book can be used as a stand-alone Training Log / Diary, it is intended to supplement the book **Kids Triathlon: The Essential Guide** by Caroline & Justin Hattee; Foreword by Vicky Holland, Olympic Bronze medallist and ITU World Champion.

Kids Triathlon: The Essential Guide: "should be the go-to manual for young, aspiring triathletes and their parents. Jam packed with tips, tricks and advice for all levels of athlete, it's perfect for the newcomer, the slightly more established youngster wanting to research a bit more or the parent trying to figure out how best to support their child(ren)." Vicky Holland.

This Training Log / Diary includes a basic explanation of what a Training Log / Dairy is and its purpose. We've then included a few sections to help you organise your training and racing life e.g. a Race Planner, Kit List and Wish Lists (everyone loves new kit!). The final section is the Training Log itself, which covers a full year of your training and racing life, allowing you to track your progress, to review and learn from in future years.

WHAT IS A
TRAINING LOG / DIARY?

Simple – it's a record of your training sessions, no more than that. But it's why you keep the log i.e. the benefits it gives you, that make it important.

You'll see that we suggest that it includes the following information, which covers the main aspects of training, together with other useful information such as the weather, how you felt and your thoughts and feelings.

DATE	01-Dec
TYPE (Swim, Bike, Run, Core, Transition)	Run (off-road)
DISTANCE	5km
TIME / DURATION	25mins
SESSION TYPE #	Easy
RPE	5
WEATHER	Windy & cold
KIT	Off-road trainers and winter clothes
INJURIES / ACHES	None before or after
GENERAL / FEELINGS / KIT	Good. Ready for a fast session next

This section can get more detailed if you're doing say, intervals or complicated swimming sets.

Adults might also include heart rate information, power data, sleep patterns and weight, but there's no need for you kids to include this information. Keep it simple!

Your log should be a source of personal pride and confidence – a clear record of your development and how much you have achieved. We're pretty sure that you have trained hard and should be proud of your development.

Read "Kids Triathlon: The Essential Guide" for information on core strength, transitions, interval training and kid friendly RPE (Rate of Perceived Effort).

WHY SHOULD YOU USE A TRAINING LOG / DIARY:

As you develop you'll find it useful to keep a record of your training sessions:

They help to motivate you:
- Showing how far you have developed; proving that all your hard work has been worthwhile!

- Giving you historic distance / speed targets to beat; so they'll help with goal setting and achievement too.

They will show how well you are progressing – or how effective your training sessions are.
- Do you need to change something if you have plateaued or continue to progress your sessions in the same way?

They will show you if you've been overtraining and can explain why you might be injured:
- If either happens to you, check your log to see if you can work out why and learn from your mistakes.
  - Have you been training too intensely, churning out too many 'junk miles' or did you increase distance/time/reps too much recently?
  - Have you been giving yourself enough recovery time? If not, your performance will stagnate (or even decline).

They can help you to get your pre-training nutrition right
- What did you eat and how long before you trained versus how you performed? It's really important to understand how your body reacts to different food types and how long your body takes to digest your food. Practise this in training and log how you perform and feel – so you'll get it right on race day.

They can help you understand how you can best plan your pre-race training (tapering) so that you perform to your potential on race day.

Your Log will also help you plan your training.
- You're a busy kid – you have school, family, friends and other interests to think about as well as training sessions. As a triathlete, you have three sets of training session to think about (five if you include 'core' and 'transition' training – and you should!). Having a log will help you to plan ahead and be organised. You can chat about what you'd like to do with your parents – get their input as well as your coaches, if you have any.

A word of caution: don't become obsessed with training. Don't let your Training Log / Diary rule your life. If you miss a session, don't worry; and don't try to make up the session tomorrow – you'll just get tired or worse.

Also, don't forget to agree with your parents / guardians where you are going and when you'll be back. Be safe.

Read "Kids Triathlon: The Essential Guide" for more details on goal setting, training progression, tapering.

RACE PLANNER

RACE NAME	TYPE*	PRIORITY**	DISTANCE	DATE	LOCATION	REGISTRATION DEADLINE	FEE	ENTERED?	GOAL	RESULT (PLACE / TOTAL)	RESULT (TIME)

*TRIATHLON, DUALATHLON, AQUATHLON, CYCLO-CROSS, CROSS-COUNTRY RUNNING, TRACK ETC
** A / B / C RACE i.e. race priority

RACE PLANNER

RACE NAME	TYPE*	PRIORITY**	DISTANCE	DATE	LOCATION	REGISTRATION DEADLINE	FEE	ENTERED?	GOAL	RESULT (PLACE / TOTAL)	RESULT (TIME)

*TRIATHLON, DUAL ATHLON, AQUATHLON, CYCLO-CROSS, CROSS-COUNTRY RUNNING, TRACK ETC
** A / B / C RACE i.e. race priority

TRI KIT CHECKLIST

Here's a handy checklist that we use to make sure we don't forget anything:

SWIM

Goggles ■

Trunks / Swimsuit / Trisuit ■

Wetsuit ■

Baby Oil ■

Plastic bag (for baby oil) ■

Swim hat (if not provided) ■

CYCLING

Bike ■

Tyres pumped ■

Bike oiled ■

In the right gear ■

Helmet ■

No. Belt or safety pins ■

T-shirt ■

Bike shoes & elastic bands ■

Elastic bands ■

Sunglasses ■

RUNNING

Trainers ■

Lube # ■

GENERAL

ID ■

Race details ■

Pre / Post race clothing ■

Pre / post race snacks ■

Water bottle* ■

Pump* ■

Spare inner tube & repair / tool kit* ■

Towel** ■

Spare trainers / flip flops*** ■

Toilet roll (in case they run out) ■

Sunscreen ■

Asthma inhaler / hayfever tablets ■

KEY

Must have ■

Open water must haves ■

Might want ■

To prevent chafing
(you have bare feet)

* In case you need them
pre-race. Don't race with
them.

** To wipe grit off your feet
(and to help you spot your
bike) - not to dry yourself.

*** To wear after you have
dropped your race trainers
in transition.

WISH LIST

MY FAVOURITE

Training sessions

_____

_____ Swim / Bike / Run

_____

_____ Swim / Bike / Run

_____

_____ Swim / Bike / Run

_____

_____ Swim / Bike / Run

_____

_____ Swim / Bike / Run

_____

_____ Swim / Bike / Run

_____

_____ Swim / Bike / Run

_____

_____ Swim / Bike / Run

_____

_____ Swim / Bike / Run

_____

_____ Swim / Bike / Run

_____

_____ Swim / Bike / Run

MY FAVOURITE

Training sessions

_____ Swim / Bike / Run

_____ Swim / Bike / Run

_____ Swim / Bike / Run

_____ Swim / Bike / Run

_____ Swim / Bike / Run

_____ Swim / Bike / Run

_____ Swim / Bike / Run

_____ Swim / Bike / Run

_____ Swim / Bike / Run

_____ Swim / Bike / Run

MY FAVOURITE

Training locations

_____

Swim / Bike / Run

_____

Swim / Bike / Run

_____

Swim / Bike / Run

_____

Swim / Bike / Run

_____

Swim / Bike / Run

_____

Swim / Bike / Run

_____

Swim / Bike / Run

_____

Swim / Bike / Run

_____

Swim / Bike / Run

_____

Swim / Bike / Run

MY FAVOURITE

Training locations

Swim / Bike / Run

Swim / Bike / Run

Swim / Bike / Run

Swim / Bike / Run

Swim / Bike / Run

Swim / Bike / Run

Swim / Bike / Run

Swim / Bike / Run

Swim / Bike / Run

Swim / Bike / Run

MY FAVOURITE

Training routes

Swim / Bike / Run

Swim / Bike / Run

Swim / Bike / Run

Swim / Bike / Run

Swim / Bike / Run

Swim / Bike / Run

Swim / Bike / Run

Swim / Bike / Run

Swim / Bike / Run

Swim / Bike / Run

Swim / Bike / Run

MY FAVOURITE

Training routes

_____ Swim / Bike / Run

_____ Swim / Bike / Run

_____ Swim / Bike / Run

_____ Swim / Bike / Run

_____ Swim / Bike / Run

_____ Swim / Bike / Run

_____ Swim / Bike / Run

_____ Swim / Bike / Run

_____ Swim / Bike / Run

_____ Swim / Bike / Run

MY FAVOURITE

Training partners

Swim / Bike / Run

Swim / Bike / Run

Swim / Bike / Run

Swim / Bike / Run

Swim / Bike / Run

Swim / Bike / Run

Swim / Bike / Run

Swim / Bike / Run

Swim / Bike / Run

Swim / Bike / Run

MY FAVOURITE

Training partners

Swim / Bike / Run

Swim / Bike / Run

Swim / Bike / Run

Swim / Bike / Run

Swim / Bike / Run

Swim / Bike / Run

Swim / Bike / Run

Swim / Bike / Run

Swim / Bike / Run

Swim / Bike / Run

TRAINING LOG

	DATE	S/B/R/C/T	DISTANCE	TIME	SESSION TYPE / DETAIL	RPE (1-10)	WEATHER	KIT	INJURIES / ACHES	GENERAL (FEELINGS / NUTRITION / KIT / ETC)
MONDAY										
TUESDAY										
WEDNESDAY										
THURSDAY										
FRIDAY										
SATURDAY										
SUNDAY										
WEEK TOTAL	/ / / / TOTAL NO.									

KEY: S - SWIM / B - BIKE / R - RUN / C - CORE STRENGTH / T - TRANSITION

Read **Kids Triathlon: The Essential Guide** for more details on kid friendly
RPE (Rate of Perceived Effort), warm ups, fun training sessions and cool downs incl. stretching.

TRAINING LOG

	DATE	S/B/R/C/T	DISTANCE	TIME	SESSION TYPE / DETAIL	RPE (1-10)	WEATHER	KIT	INJURIES / ACHES	GENERAL (FEELINGS / NUTRITION / KIT / ETC)
MONDAY										
TUESDAY										
WEDNESDAY										
THURSDAY										
FRIDAY										
SATURDAY										
SUNDAY										
WEEK TOTAL	/ / / / TOTAL NO.									

KEY: S - SWIM / B - BIKE / R - RUN / C - CORE STRENGTH / T - TRANSITION

Read **Kids Triathlon: The Essential Guide** for more details on kid friendly
RPE (Rate of Perceived Effort), warm ups, fun training sessions and cool downs incl. stretching.

TRAINING LOG

	DATE	S/B/R/C/T	DISTANCE	TIME	SESSION TYPE / DETAIL	RPE (1-10)	WEATHER	KIT	INJURIES / ACHES	GENERAL (FEELINGS / NUTRITION / KIT / ETC)
MONDAY										
TUESDAY										
WEDNESDAY										
THURSDAY										
FRIDAY										
SATURDAY										
SUNDAY										
WEEK TOTAL	/ / / / TOTAL NO.									

KEY: S - SWIM / B - BIKE / R - RUN / C - CORE STRENGTH / T - TRANSITION

Read **Kids Triathlon: The Essential Guide** for more details on kid friendly RPE (Rate of Perceived Effort), warm ups, fun training sessions and cool downs incl. stretching.

TRAINING LOG

DATE	S/B/R/C/T	DISTANCE	TIME	SESSION TYPE / DETAIL	RPE (1-10)	WEATHER	KIT	INJURIES / ACHES	GENERAL (FEELINGS / NUTRITION / KIT / ETC)
MONDAY									
TUESDAY									
WEDNESDAY									
THURSDAY									
FRIDAY									
SATURDAY									
SUNDAY									
WEEK TOTAL	/ / / / TOTAL NO.								

KEY: S - SWIM / B - BIKE / R - RUN / C - CORE STRENGTH / T - TRANSITION

Read **Kids Triathlon: The Essential Guide** for more details on kid friendly
RPE (Rate of Perceived Effort), warm ups, fun training sessions and cool downs incl. stretching.

TRAINING LOG

	DATE	S/B/R/C/T	DISTANCE	TIME	SESSION TYPE / DETAIL	RPE (1-10)	WEATHER	KIT	INJURIES / ACHES	GENERAL (FEELINGS / NUTRITION / KIT / ETC)
MONDAY										
TUESDAY										
WEDNESDAY										
THURSDAY										
FRIDAY										
SATURDAY										
SUNDAY										
WEEK TOTAL	/ / / / TOTAL NO.									

KEY: S - SWIM / B - BIKE / R - RUN / C - CORE STRENGTH / T - TRANSITION

Read **Kids Triathlon: The Essential Guide** for more details on kid friendly
RPE (Rate of Perceived Effort), warm ups, fun training sessions and cool downs incl. stretching.

TRAINING LOG

	DATE	S/B/R/C/T	DISTANCE	TIME	SESSION TYPE / DETAIL	RPE (1-10)	WEATHER	KIT	INJURIES / ACHES	GENERAL (FEELINGS / NUTRITION / KIT / ETC)
MONDAY										
TUESDAY										
WEDNESDAY										
THURSDAY										
FRIDAY										
SATURDAY										
SUNDAY										
WEEK TOTAL	/ / / / TOTAL NO.									

KEY: S - SWIM / B - BIKE / R - RUN / C - CORE STRENGTH / T - TRANSITION

Read **Kids Triathlon: The Essential Guide** for more details on kid friendly
RPE (Rate of Perceived Effort), warm ups, fun training sessions and cool downs incl. stretching.

TRAINING LOG

	DATE	S/B/R/C/T	DISTANCE	TIME	SESSION TYPE / DETAIL	RPE (1-10)	WEATHER	KIT	INJURIES / ACHES	GENERAL (FEELINGS / NUTRITION / KIT / ETC)
MONDAY										
TUESDAY										
WEDNESDAY										
THURSDAY										
FRIDAY										
SATURDAY										
SUNDAY										
WEEK TOTAL	/ / / / TOTAL NO.									

KEY: S - SWIM / B - BIKE / R - RUN / C - CORE STRENGTH / T - TRANSITION

Read **Kids Triathlon: The Essential Guide** for more details on kid friendly
RPE (Rate of Perceived Effort), warm ups, fun training sessions and cool downs incl. stretching.

TRAINING LOG

DATE	S/B/R/C/T	DISTANCE	TIME	SESSION TYPE / DETAIL	RPE (1-10)	WEATHER	KIT	INJURIES / ACHES	GENERAL (FEELINGS / NUTRITION / KIT / ETC)
MONDAY									
TUESDAY									
WEDNESDAY									
THURSDAY									
FRIDAY									
SATURDAY									
SUNDAY									
WEEK TOTAL	/ / / / TOTAL NO.								

KEY: S - SWIM / B - BIKE / R - RUN / C - CORE STRENGTH / T - TRANSITION

Read **Kids Triathlon: The Essential Guide** for more details on kid friendly
RPE (Rate of Perceived Effort), warm ups, fun training sessions and cool downs incl. stretching.

TRAINING LOG

	DATE	S/B/R/C/T	DISTANCE	TIME	SESSION TYPE / DETAIL	RPE (1-10)	WEATHER	KIT	INJURIES / ACHES	GENERAL (FEELINGS / NUTRITION / KIT / ETC)
MONDAY										
TUESDAY										
WEDNESDAY										
THURSDAY										
FRIDAY										
SATURDAY										
SUNDAY										
WEEK TOTAL	/ / / / TOTAL NO.									

KEY: S - SWIM / B - BIKE / R - RUN / C - CORE STRENGTH / T - TRANSITION

Read **Kids Triathlon: The Essential Guide** for more details on kid friendly
RPE (Rate of Perceived Effort), warm ups, fun training sessions and cool downs incl. stretching.

TRAINING LOG

DATE	S/B/R/C/T	DISTANCE	TIME	SESSION TYPE / DETAIL	RPE (1-10)	WEATHER	KIT	INJURIES / ACHES	GENERAL (FEELINGS / NUTRITION / KIT / ETC)
MONDAY									
TUESDAY									
WEDNESDAY									
THURSDAY									
FRIDAY									
SATURDAY									
SUNDAY									
WEEK TOTAL	/ / / / TOTAL NO.								

KEY: S - SWIM / B - BIKE / R - RUN / C - CORE STRENGTH / T - TRANSITION

Read **Kids Triathlon: The Essential Guide** for more details on kid friendly
RPE (Rate of Perceived Effort), warm ups, fun training sessions and cool downs incl. stretching.

TRAINING LOG

	DATE	S/B/R/C/T	DISTANCE	TIME	SESSION TYPE / DETAIL	RPE (1-10)	WEATHER	KIT	INJURIES / ACHES	GENERAL (FEELINGS / NUTRITION / KIT / ETC)
MONDAY										
TUESDAY										
WEDNESDAY										
THURSDAY										
FRIDAY										
SATURDAY										
SUNDAY										
WEEK TOTAL	/ / / / TOTAL NO.									

KEY: S - SWIM / B - BIKE / R - RUN / C - CORE STRENGTH / T - TRANSITION

Read **Kids Triathlon: The Essential Guide** for more details on kid friendly
RPE (Rate of Perceived Effort), warm ups, fun training sessions and cool downs incl. stretching.

TRAINING LOG

DATE	S/B/R/C/T	DISTANCE	TIME	SESSION TYPE / DETAIL	RPE (1-10)	WEATHER	KIT	INJURIES / ACHES	GENERAL (FEELINGS / NUTRITION / KIT / ETC)
MONDAY									
TUESDAY									
WEDNESDAY									
THURSDAY									
FRIDAY									
SATURDAY									
SUNDAY									
WEEK TOTAL	/ / / / TOTAL NO.								

KEY: S - SWIM / B - BIKE / R - RUN / C - CORE STRENGTH / T - TRANSITION

Read **Kids Triathlon: The Essential Guide** for more details on kid friendly
RPE (Rate of Perceived Effort), warm ups, fun training sessions and cool downs incl. stretching.

TRAINING LOG

DATE	S/B/R/C/T	DISTANCE	TIME	SESSION TYPE / DETAIL	RPE (1-10)	WEATHER	KIT	INJURIES / ACHES	GENERAL (FEELINGS / NUTRITION / KIT / ETC)
MONDAY									
TUESDAY									
WEDNESDAY									
THURSDAY									
FRIDAY									
SATURDAY									
SUNDAY									
WEEK TOTAL	/ / / / TOTAL NO.								

KEY: S - SWIM / B - BIKE / R - RUN / C - CORE STRENGTH / T - TRANSITION

Read **Kids Triathlon: The Essential Guide** for more details on kid friendly
RPE (Rate of Perceived Effort), warm ups, fun training sessions and cool downs incl. stretching.

TRAINING LOG

	DATE	S/B/R/C/T	DISTANCE	TIME	SESSION TYPE / DETAIL	RPE (1-10)	WEATHER	KIT	INJURIES / ACHES	GENERAL (FEELINGS / NUTRITION / KIT / ETC)
MONDAY										
TUESDAY										
WEDNESDAY										
THURSDAY										
FRIDAY										
SATURDAY										
SUNDAY										
WEEK TOTAL	/ / / / TOTAL NO.									

KEY: S - SWIM / B - BIKE / R - RUN / C - CORE STRENGTH / T - TRANSITION

Read **Kids Triathlon: The Essential Guide** for more details on kid friendly
RPE (Rate of Perceived Effort), warm ups, fun training sessions and cool downs incl. stretching.

TRAINING LOG

	DATE	S/B/R/C/T	DISTANCE	TIME	SESSION TYPE / DETAIL	RPE (1-10)	WEATHER	KIT	INJURIES / ACHES	GENERAL (FEELINGS / NUTRITION / KIT / ETC)
MONDAY										
TUESDAY										
WEDNESDAY										
THURSDAY										
FRIDAY										
SATURDAY										
SUNDAY										
WEEK TOTAL	/ / / / TOTAL NO.									

KEY: S - SWIM / B - BIKE / R - RUN / C - CORE STRENGTH / T - TRANSITION

Read **Kids Triathlon: The Essential Guide** for more details on kid friendly
RPE (Rate of Perceived Effort), warm ups, fun training sessions and cool downs incl. stretching.

TRAINING LOG

	DATE	S/B/R/C/T	DISTANCE	TIME	SESSION TYPE / DETAIL	RPE (1-10)	WEATHER	KIT	INJURIES / ACHES	GENERAL (FEELINGS / NUTRITION / KIT / ETC)
MONDAY										
TUESDAY										
WEDNESDAY										
THURSDAY										
FRIDAY										
SATURDAY										
SUNDAY										
WEEK TOTAL	/ / / / TOTAL NO.									

KEY: S - SWIM / B - BIKE / R - RUN / C - CORE STRENGTH / T - TRANSITION

Read **Kids Triathlon: The Essential Guide** for more details on kid friendly RPE (Rate of Perceived Effort), warm ups, fun training sessions and cool downs incl. stretching.

TRAINING LOG

	DATE	S/B/R/C/T	DISTANCE	TIME	SESSION TYPE / DETAIL	RPE (1-10)	WEATHER	KIT	INJURIES / ACHES	GENERAL (FEELINGS / NUTRITION / KIT / ETC)
MONDAY										
TUESDAY										
WEDNESDAY										
THURSDAY										
FRIDAY										
SATURDAY										
SUNDAY										
WEEK TOTAL	/ / / / TOTAL NO.									

KEY: S - SWIM / B - BIKE / R - RUN / C - CORE STRENGTH / T - TRANSITION

Read **Kids Triathlon: The Essential Guide** for more details on kid friendly
RPE (Rate of Perceived Effort), warm ups, fun training sessions and cool downs incl. stretching.

TRAINING LOG

DATE	S/B/R/C/T	DISTANCE	TIME	SESSION TYPE / DETAIL	RPE (1-10)	WEATHER	KIT	INJURIES / ACHES	GENERAL (FEELINGS / NUTRITION / KIT / ETC)
MONDAY									
TUESDAY									
WEDNESDAY									
THURSDAY									
FRIDAY									
SATURDAY									
SUNDAY									
WEEK TOTAL	/ / / / TOTAL NO.								

KEY: S - SWIM / B - BIKE / R - RUN / C - CORE STRENGTH / T - TRANSITION

Read **Kids Triathlon: The Essential Guide** for more details on kid friendly
RPE (Rate of Perceived Effort), warm ups, fun training sessions and cool downs incl. stretching.

TRAINING LOG

DATE	S/B/R/C/T	DISTANCE	TIME	SESSION TYPE / DETAIL	RPE (1-10)	WEATHER	KIT	INJURIES / ACHES	GENERAL (FEELINGS / NUTRITION / KIT / ETC)
MONDAY									
TUESDAY									
WEDNESDAY									
THURSDAY									
FRIDAY									
SATURDAY									
SUNDAY									
WEEK TOTAL	/ / / / TOTAL NO. ········								

KEY: S - SWIM / B - BIKE / R - RUN / C - CORE STRENGTH / T - TRANSITION

Read **Kids Triathlon: The Essential Guide** for more details on kid friendly
RPE (Rate of Perceived Effort), warm ups, fun training sessions and cool downs incl. stretching.

TRAINING LOG

	DATE	S/B/R/C/T	DISTANCE	TIME	SESSION TYPE / DETAIL	RPE (1-10)	WEATHER	KIT	INJURIES / ACHES	GENERAL (FEELINGS / NUTRITION / KIT / ETC)
MONDAY										
TUESDAY										
WEDNESDAY										
THURSDAY										
FRIDAY										
SATURDAY										
SUNDAY										
WEEK TOTAL	/ / / / TOTAL NO.									

KEY: S - SWIM / B - BIKE / R - RUN / C - CORE STRENGTH / T - TRANSITION

Read **Kids Triathlon: The Essential Guide** for more details on kid friendly RPE (Rate of Perceived Effort), warm ups, fun training sessions and cool downs incl. stretching.

TRAINING LOG

	DATE	S/B/R/C/T	DISTANCE	TIME	SESSION TYPE / DETAIL	RPE (1-10)	WEATHER	KIT	INJURIES / ACHES	GENERAL (FEELINGS / NUTRITION / KIT / ETC)
MONDAY										
TUESDAY										
WEDNESDAY										
THURSDAY										
FRIDAY										
SATURDAY										
SUNDAY										
WEEK TOTAL	/ / / / TOTAL NO.									

KEY: S - SWIM / B - BIKE / R - RUN / C - CORE STRENGTH / T - TRANSITION

Read **Kids Triathlon: The Essential Guide** for more details on kid friendly
RPE (Rate of Perceived Effort), warm ups, fun training sessions and cool downs incl. stretching.

TRAINING LOG

	DATE	S/B/R/C/T	DISTANCE	TIME	SESSION TYPE / DETAIL	RPE (1-10)	WEATHER	KIT	INJURIES / ACHES	GENERAL (FEELINGS / NUTRITION / KIT / ETC)
MONDAY										
TUESDAY										
WEDNESDAY										
THURSDAY										
FRIDAY										
SATURDAY										
SUNDAY										
WEEK TOTAL	/ / / / TOTAL NO.									

KEY: S - SWIM / B - BIKE / R - RUN / C - CORE STRENGTH / T - TRANSITION

Read **Kids Triathlon: The Essential Guide** for more details on kid friendly
RPE (Rate of Perceived Effort), warm ups, fun training sessions and cool downs incl. stretching.

TRAINING LOG

	DATE	S/B/R/C/T	DISTANCE	TIME	SESSION TYPE / DETAIL	RPE (1-10)	WEATHER	KIT	INJURIES / ACHES	GENERAL (FEELINGS / NUTRITION / KIT / ETC)
MONDAY										
TUESDAY										
WEDNESDAY										
THURSDAY										
FRIDAY										
SATURDAY										
SUNDAY										
WEEK TOTAL	/ / / / TOTAL NO.									

KEY: S - SWIM / B - BIKE / R - RUN / C - CORE STRENGTH / T - TRANSITION

Read **Kids Triathlon: The Essential Guide** for more details on kid friendly RPE (Rate of Perceived Effort), warm ups, fun training sessions and cool downs incl. stretching.

TRAINING LOG

	DATE	S/B/R/C/T	DISTANCE	TIME	SESSION TYPE / DETAIL	RPE (1-10)	WEATHER	KIT	INJURIES / ACHES	GENERAL (FEELINGS / NUTRITION / KIT / ETC)
MONDAY										
TUESDAY										
WEDNESDAY										
THURSDAY										
FRIDAY										
SATURDAY										
SUNDAY										
WEEK TOTAL	/ / / / TOTAL NO.									

KEY: S - SWIM / B - BIKE / R - RUN / C - CORE STRENGTH / T - TRANSITION

Read **Kids Triathlon: The Essential Guide** for more details on kid friendly
RPE (Rate of Perceived Effort), warm ups, fun training sessions and cool downs incl. stretching.

TRAINING LOG

	DATE	S/B/R/C/T	DISTANCE	TIME	SESSION TYPE / DETAIL	RPE (1-10)	WEATHER	KIT	INJURIES / ACHES	GENERAL (FEELINGS / NUTRITION / KIT / ETC)
MONDAY										
TUESDAY										
WEDNESDAY										
THURSDAY										
FRIDAY										
SATURDAY										
SUNDAY										
WEEK TOTAL	/ / / / TOTAL NO.									

KEY: S - SWIM / B - BIKE / R - RUN / C - CORE STRENGTH / T - TRANSITION

Read **Kids Triathlon: The Essential Guide** for more details on kid friendly
RPE (Rate of Perceived Effort), warm ups, fun training sessions and cool downs incl. stretching.

TRAINING LOG

	DATE	S/B/R/C/T	DISTANCE	TIME	SESSION TYPE / DETAIL	RPE (1-10)	WEATHER	KIT	INJURIES / ACHES	GENERAL (FEELINGS / NUTRITION / KIT / ETC)
MONDAY										
TUESDAY										
WEDNESDAY										
THURSDAY										
FRIDAY										
SATURDAY										
SUNDAY										
WEEK TOTAL	/ / / / TOTAL NO.									

KEY: S - SWIM / B - BIKE / R - RUN / C - CORE STRENGTH / T - TRANSITION

Read **Kids Triathlon: The Essential Guide** for more details on kid friendly
RPE (Rate of Perceived Effort), warm ups, fun training sessions and cool downs incl. stretching.

TRAINING LOG

	DATE	S/B/R/C/T	DISTANCE	TIME	SESSION TYPE / DETAIL	RPE (1-10)	WEATHER	KIT	INJURIES / ACHES	GENERAL (FEELINGS / NUTRITION / KIT / ETC)
MONDAY										
TUESDAY										
WEDNESDAY										
THURSDAY										
FRIDAY										
SATURDAY										
SUNDAY										
WEEK TOTAL	/ / / / TOTAL NO.									

KEY: S - SWIM / B - BIKE / R - RUN / C - CORE STRENGTH / T - TRANSITION

Read **Kids Triathlon: The Essential Guide** for more details on kid friendly
RPE (Rate of Perceived Effort), warm ups, fun training sessions and cool downs incl. stretching.

TRAINING LOG

	DATE	S/B/R/C/T	DISTANCE	TIME	SESSION TYPE / DETAIL	RPE (1-10)	WEATHER	KIT	INJURIES / ACHES	GENERAL (FEELINGS / NUTRITION / KIT / ETC)
MONDAY										
TUESDAY										
WEDNESDAY										
THURSDAY										
FRIDAY										
SATURDAY										
SUNDAY										
WEEK TOTAL	/ / / / TOTAL NO.									

KEY: S - SWIM / B - BIKE / R - RUN / C - CORE STRENGTH / T - TRANSITION

Read **Kids Triathlon: The Essential Guide** for more details on kid friendly
RPE (Rate of Perceived Effort), warm ups, fun training sessions and cool downs incl. stretching.

TRAINING LOG

	DATE	S/B/R/C/T	DISTANCE	TIME	SESSION TYPE / DETAIL	RPE (1-10)	WEATHER	KIT	INJURIES / ACHES	GENERAL (FEELINGS / NUTRITION / KIT / ETC)
MONDAY										
TUESDAY										
WEDNESDAY										
THURSDAY										
FRIDAY										
SATURDAY										
SUNDAY										
WEEK TOTAL		/ / / / TOTAL NO.								

KEY: S - SWIM / B - BIKE / R - RUN / C - CORE STRENGTH / T - TRANSITION

Read **Kids Triathlon: The Essential Guide** for more details on kid friendly
RPE (Rate of Perceived Effort), warm ups, fun training sessions and cool downs incl. stretching.

TRAINING LOG

	DATE	S/B/R/C/T	DISTANCE	TIME	SESSION TYPE / DETAIL	RPE (1-10)	WEATHER	KIT	INJURIES / ACHES	GENERAL (FEELINGS / NUTRITION / KIT / ETC)
MONDAY										
TUESDAY										
WEDNESDAY										
THURSDAY										
FRIDAY										
SATURDAY										
SUNDAY										
WEEK TOTAL	/ / / / TOTAL NO.									

KEY: S - SWIM / B - BIKE / R - RUN / C - CORE STRENGTH / T - TRANSITION

Read **Kids Triathlon: The Essential Guide** for more details on kid friendly RPE (Rate of Perceived Effort), warm ups, fun training sessions and cool downs incl. stretching.

TRAINING LOG

	DATE	S/B/R/C/T	DISTANCE	TIME	SESSION TYPE / DETAIL	RPE (1-10)	WEATHER	KIT	INJURIES / ACHES	GENERAL (FEELINGS / NUTRITION / KIT / ETC)
MONDAY										
TUESDAY										
WEDNESDAY										
THURSDAY										
FRIDAY										
SATURDAY										
SUNDAY										
WEEK TOTAL	/ / / / TOTAL NO.									

KEY: S - SWIM / B - BIKE / R - RUN / C - CORE STRENGTH / T - TRANSITION

Read **Kids Triathlon: The Essential Guide** for more details on kid friendly
RPE (Rate of Perceived Effort), warm ups, fun training sessions and cool downs incl. stretching.

TRAINING LOG

	DATE	S/B/R/C/T	DISTANCE	TIME	SESSION TYPE / DETAIL	RPE (1-10)	WEATHER	KIT	INJURIES / ACHES	GENERAL (FEELINGS / NUTRITION / KIT / ETC)
MONDAY										
TUESDAY										
WEDNESDAY										
THURSDAY										
FRIDAY										
SATURDAY										
SUNDAY										
WEEK TOTAL	/ / / / TOTAL NO.									

KEY: S - SWIM / B - BIKE / R - RUN / C - CORE STRENGTH / T - TRANSITION

Read **Kids Triathlon: The Essential Guide** for more details on kid friendly
RPE (Rate of Perceived Effort), warm ups, fun training sessions and cool downs incl. stretching.

TRAINING LOG

DATE	S/B/R/C/T	DISTANCE	TIME	SESSION TYPE / DETAIL	RPE (1-10)	WEATHER	KIT	INJURIES / ACHES	GENERAL (FEELINGS / NUTRITION / KIT / ETC)
MONDAY									
TUESDAY									
WEDNESDAY									
THURSDAY									
FRIDAY									
SATURDAY									
SUNDAY									
WEEK TOTAL	/ / / / TOTAL NO.								

KEY: S - SWIM / B - BIKE / R - RUN / C - CORE STRENGTH / T - TRANSITION

Read **Kids Triathlon: The Essential Guide** for more details on kid friendly
RPE (Rate of Perceived Effort), warm ups, fun training sessions and cool downs incl. stretching.

TRAINING LOG

	DATE	S/B/R/C/T	DISTANCE	TIME	SESSION TYPE / DETAIL	RPE (1-10)	WEATHER	KIT	INJURIES / ACHES	GENERAL (FEELINGS / NUTRITION / KIT / ETC)
MONDAY										
TUESDAY										
WEDNESDAY										
THURSDAY										
FRIDAY										
SATURDAY										
SUNDAY										
WEEK TOTAL	/ / / / TOTAL NO.									

KEY: S - SWIM / B - BIKE / R - RUN / C - CORE STRENGTH / T - TRANSITION

Read **Kids Triathlon: The Essential Guide** for more details on kid friendly
RPE (Rate of Perceived Effort), warm ups, fun training sessions and cool downs incl. stretching.

TRAINING LOG

	DATE	S/B/R/C/T	DISTANCE	TIME	SESSION TYPE / DETAIL	RPE (1-10)	WEATHER	KIT	INJURIES / ACHES	GENERAL (FEELINGS / NUTRITION / KIT / ETC)
MONDAY										
TUESDAY										
WEDNESDAY										
THURSDAY										
FRIDAY										
SATURDAY										
SUNDAY										
WEEK TOTAL	TOTAL NO. / / / /									

KEY: S - SWIM / B - BIKE / R - RUN / C - CORE STRENGTH / T - TRANSITION

Read **Kids Triathlon: The Essential Guide** for more details on kid friendly
RPE (Rate of Perceived Effort), warm ups, fun training sessions and cool downs incl. stretching.

TRAINING LOG

	DATE	S/B/R/C/T	DISTANCE	TIME	SESSION TYPE / DETAIL	RPE (1-10)	WEATHER	KIT	INJURIES / ACHES	GENERAL (FEELINGS / NUTRITION / KIT / ETC)
MONDAY										
TUESDAY										
WEDNESDAY										
THURSDAY										
FRIDAY										
SATURDAY										
SUNDAY										
WEEK TOTAL	/ / / / TOTAL NO.									

KEY: S - SWIM / B - BIKE / R - RUN / C - CORE STRENGTH / T - TRANSITION

Read **Kids Triathlon: The Essential Guide** for more details on kid friendly
RPE (Rate of Perceived Effort), warm ups, fun training sessions and cool downs incl. stretching.

TRAINING LOG

DATE	S/B/R/C/T	DISTANCE	TIME	SESSION TYPE / DETAIL	RPE (1-10)	WEATHER	KIT	INJURIES / ACHES	GENERAL (FEELINGS / NUTRITION / KIT / ETC)
MONDAY									
TUESDAY									
WEDNESDAY									
THURSDAY									
FRIDAY									
SATURDAY									
SUNDAY									
WEEK TOTAL	/ / / / TOTAL NO.								

KEY: S - SWIM / B - BIKE / R - RUN / C - CORE STRENGTH / T - TRANSITION

Read **Kids Triathlon: The Essential Guide** for more details on kid friendly
RPE (Rate of Perceived Effort), warm ups, fun training sessions and cool downs incl. stretching.

TRAINING LOG

DATE	S/B/R/C/T	DISTANCE	TIME	SESSION TYPE / DETAIL	RPE (1-10)	WEATHER	KIT	INJURIES / ACHES	GENERAL (FEELINGS / NUTRITION / KIT / ETC)
MONDAY									
TUESDAY									
WEDNESDAY									
THURSDAY									
FRIDAY									
SATURDAY									
SUNDAY									
WEEK TOTAL	/ / / / TOTAL NO.								

KEY: S - SWIM / B - BIKE / R - RUN / C - CORE STRENGTH / T - TRANSITION

Read **Kids Triathlon: The Essential Guide** for more details on kid friendly
RPE (Rate of Perceived Effort), warm ups, fun training sessions and cool downs incl. stretching.

TRAINING LOG

DATE	S/B/R/C/T	DISTANCE	TIME	SESSION TYPE / DETAIL	RPE (1-10)	WEATHER	KIT	INJURIES / ACHES	GENERAL (FEELINGS / NUTRITION / KIT / ETC)
MONDAY									
TUESDAY									
WEDNESDAY									
THURSDAY									
FRIDAY									
SATURDAY									
SUNDAY									
WEEK TOTAL	/ / / / TOTAL NO.								

KEY: S - SWIM / B - BIKE / R - RUN / C - CORE STRENGTH / T - TRANSITION

Read **Kids Triathlon: The Essential Guide** for more details on kid friendly
RPE (Rate of Perceived Effort), warm ups, fun training sessions and cool downs incl. stretching.

TRAINING LOG

	DATE	S/B/R/C/T	DISTANCE	TIME	SESSION TYPE / DETAIL	RPE (1-10)	WEATHER	KIT	INJURIES / ACHES	GENERAL (FEELINGS / NUTRITION / KIT / ETC)
MONDAY										
TUESDAY										
WEDNESDAY										
THURSDAY										
FRIDAY										
SATURDAY										
SUNDAY										
WEEK TOTAL	/ / / / TOTAL NO.									

KEY: S - SWIM / B - BIKE / R - RUN / C - CORE STRENGTH / T - TRANSITION

Read **Kids Triathlon: The Essential Guide** for more details on kid friendly
RPE (Rate of Perceived Effort), warm ups, fun training sessions and cool downs incl. stretching.

TRAINING LOG

	DATE	S/B/R/C/T	DISTANCE	TIME	SESSION TYPE / DETAIL	RPE (1-10)	WEATHER	KIT	INJURIES / ACHES	GENERAL (FEELINGS / NUTRITION / KIT / ETC)
MONDAY										
TUESDAY										
WEDNESDAY										
THURSDAY										
FRIDAY										
SATURDAY										
SUNDAY										
WEEK TOTAL	/ / / / TOTAL NO.									

KEY: S - SWIM / B - BIKE / R - RUN / C - CORE STRENGTH / T - TRANSITION

Read **Kids Triathlon: The Essential Guide** for more details on kid friendly
RPE (Rate of Perceived Effort), warm ups, fun training sessions and cool downs incl. stretching.

TRAINING LOG

DATE	S/B/R/C/T	DISTANCE	TIME	SESSION TYPE / DETAIL	RPE (1-10)	WEATHER	KIT	INJURIES / ACHES	GENERAL (FEELINGS / NUTRITION / KIT / ETC)
MONDAY									
TUESDAY									
WEDNESDAY									
THURSDAY									
FRIDAY									
SATURDAY									
SUNDAY									
WEEK TOTAL	/ / / / TOTAL NO.								

KEY: S - SWIM / B - BIKE / R - RUN / C - CORE STRENGTH / T - TRANSITION

Read **Kids Triathlon: The Essential Guide** for more details on kid friendly
RPE (Rate of Perceived Effort), warm ups, fun training sessions and cool downs incl. stretching.

TRAINING LOG

	DATE	S/B/R/C/T	DISTANCE	TIME	SESSION TYPE / DETAIL	RPE (1-10)	WEATHER	KIT	INJURIES / ACHES	GENERAL (FEELINGS / NUTRITION / KIT / ETC)
MONDAY										
TUESDAY										
WEDNESDAY										
THURSDAY										
FRIDAY										
SATURDAY										
SUNDAY										
WEEK TOTAL	/ / / / TOTAL NO.									

KEY: S - SWIM / B - BIKE / R - RUN / C - CORE STRENGTH / T - TRANSITION

Read **Kids Triathlon: The Essential Guide** for more details on kid friendly
RPE (Rate of Perceived Effort), warm ups, fun training sessions and cool downs incl. stretching.

TRAINING LOG

DATE	S/B/R/C/T	DISTANCE	TIME	SESSION TYPE / DETAIL	RPE (1-10)	WEATHER	KIT	INJURIES / ACHES	GENERAL (FEELINGS / NUTRITION / KIT / ETC)
MONDAY									
TUESDAY									
WEDNESDAY									
THURSDAY									
FRIDAY									
SATURDAY									
SUNDAY									
WEEK TOTAL	/ / / / TOTAL NO.								

KEY: S - SWIM / B - BIKE / R - RUN / C - CORE STRENGTH / T - TRANSITION

Read **Kids Triathlon: The Essential Guide** for more details on kid friendly
RPE (Rate of Perceived Effort), warm ups, fun training sessions and cool downs incl. stretching.

TRAINING LOG

	DATE	S/B/R/C/T	DISTANCE	TIME	SESSION TYPE / DETAIL	RPE (1-10)	WEATHER	KIT	INJURIES / ACHES	GENERAL (FEELINGS / NUTRITION / KIT / ETC)
MONDAY										
TUESDAY										
WEDNESDAY										
THURSDAY										
FRIDAY										
SATURDAY										
SUNDAY										
WEEK TOTAL	//// TOTAL NO.									

KEY: S - SWIM / B - BIKE / R - RUN / C - CORE STRENGTH / T - TRANSITION

Read **Kids Triathlon: The Essential Guide** for more details on kid friendly
RPE (Rate of Perceived Effort), warm ups, fun training sessions and cool downs incl. stretching.

TRAINING LOG

DATE	S/B/R/C/T	DISTANCE	TIME	SESSION TYPE / DETAIL	RPE (1-10)	WEATHER	KIT	INJURIES / ACHES	GENERAL (FEELINGS / NUTRITION / KIT / ETC)
MONDAY									
TUESDAY									
WEDNESDAY									
THURSDAY									
FRIDAY									
SATURDAY									
SUNDAY									
WEEK TOTAL	/ / / / TOTAL NO.								

KEY: S - SWIM / B - BIKE / R - RUN / C - CORE STRENGTH / T - TRANSITION

Read **Kids Triathlon: The Essential Guide** for more details on kid friendly
RPE (Rate of Perceived Effort), warm ups, fun training sessions and cool downs incl. stretching.

TRAINING LOG

	DATE	S/B/R/C/T	DISTANCE	TIME	SESSION TYPE / DETAIL	RPE (1-10)	WEATHER	KIT	INJURIES / ACHES	GENERAL (FEELINGS / NUTRITION / KIT / ETC)
MONDAY										
TUESDAY										
WEDNESDAY										
THURSDAY										
FRIDAY										
SATURDAY										
SUNDAY										
WEEK TOTAL	/ / / / TOTAL NO.									

KEY: S - SWIM / B - BIKE / R - RUN / C - CORE STRENGTH / T - TRANSITION

Read **Kids Triathlon: The Essential Guide** for more details on kid friendly
RPE (Rate of Perceived Effort), warm ups, fun training sessions and cool downs incl. stretching.

TRAINING LOG

DATE	S/B/R/C/T	DISTANCE	TIME	SESSION TYPE / DETAIL	RPE (1-10)	WEATHER	KIT	INJURIES / ACHES	GENERAL (FEELINGS / NUTRITION / KIT / ETC)
MONDAY									
TUESDAY									
WEDNESDAY									
THURSDAY									
FRIDAY									
SATURDAY									
SUNDAY									
WEEK TOTAL	/ / / / TOTAL NO.								

KEY: S - SWIM / B - BIKE / R - RUN / C - CORE STRENGTH / T - TRANSITION

Read **Kids Triathlon: The Essential Guide** for more details on kid friendly
RPE (Rate of Perceived Effort), warm ups, fun training sessions and cool downs incl. stretching.

TRAINING LOG

	DATE	S/B/R/C/T	DISTANCE	TIME	SESSION TYPE / DETAIL	RPE (1-10)	WEATHER	KIT	INJURIES / ACHES	GENERAL (FEELINGS / NUTRITION / KIT / ETC)
MONDAY										
TUESDAY										
WEDNESDAY										
THURSDAY										
FRIDAY										
SATURDAY										
SUNDAY										
WEEK TOTAL	/ / / / TOTAL NO.									

KEY: S - SWIM / B - BIKE / R - RUN / C - CORE STRENGTH / T - TRANSITION

Read **Kids Triathlon: The Essential Guide** for more details on kid friendly
RPE (Rate of Perceived Effort), warm ups, fun training sessions and cool downs incl. stretching.

TRAINING LOG

DATE	S/B/R/C/T	DISTANCE	TIME	SESSION TYPE / DETAIL	RPE (1-10)	WEATHER	KIT	INJURIES / ACHES	GENERAL (FEELINGS / NUTRITION / KIT / ETC)
MONDAY									
TUESDAY									
WEDNESDAY									
THURSDAY									
FRIDAY									
SATURDAY									
SUNDAY									
WEEK TOTAL	/ / / / TOTAL NO.								

KEY: S - SWIM / B - BIKE / R - RUN / C - CORE STRENGTH / T - TRANSITION

Read **Kids Triathlon: The Essential Guide** for more details on kid friendly
RPE (Rate of Perceived Effort), warm ups, fun training sessions and cool downs incl. stretching.

TRAINING LOG

DATE	S/B/R/C/T	DISTANCE	TIME	SESSION TYPE / DETAIL	RPE (1-10)	WEATHER	KIT	INJURIES / ACHES	GENERAL (FEELINGS / NUTRITION / KIT / ETC)
MONDAY									
TUESDAY									
WEDNESDAY									
THURSDAY									
FRIDAY									
SATURDAY									
SUNDAY									
WEEK TOTAL	/ / / / TOTAL NO.								

KEY: S - SWIM / B - BIKE / R - RUN / C - CORE STRENGTH / T - TRANSITION

Read **Kids Triathlon: The Essential Guide** for more details on kid friendly
RPE (Rate of Perceived Effort), warm ups, fun training sessions and cool downs incl. stretching.

TRAINING LOG

DATE	S/B/R/C/T	DISTANCE	TIME	SESSION TYPE / DETAIL	RPE (1-10)	WEATHER	KIT	INJURIES / ACHES	GENERAL (FEELINGS / NUTRITION / KIT / ETC)
MONDAY									
TUESDAY									
WEDNESDAY									
THURSDAY									
FRIDAY									
SATURDAY									
SUNDAY									
WEEK TOTAL	/ / / / TOTAL NO.								

KEY: S - SWIM / B - BIKE / R - RUN / C - CORE STRENGTH / T - TRANSITION

Read **Kids Triathlon: The Essential Guide** for more details on kid friendly
RPE (Rate of Perceived Effort), warm ups, fun training sessions and cool downs incl. stretching.

NOTES

NOTES

ABOUT THE AUTHORS

Caroline and Justin have a combined 35 years triathlon 'racing' experience, albeit at a level significantly below 'elite'. Despite numerous injuries they came to realise that sheer talent (the lack of) was holding them back (together with full time jobs and two kids), and resolved to start a kids' triathlon club to support their local community.

'Ketton Panthers', spurred on by the glory of the London Olympics, was established in 2012 on a quiet lane outside their home in Rutland, England. Word spread quickly and when 30 kids turned up they realised that they'd upset the neighbours if they kept closing the road. Moving to the local sports centre, obtaining British Triathlon coaching certificates, and benefiting from the superb support of coaches, committee members and parents alike (all giving freely of their time) the club expanded quickly to over 150 members and gradually took over their lives. The club now also runs a 'Minis' group (for 4 – 7 year olds), an 'Academy' (for older, developing triathletes) and sessions for kids with Downs Syndrome and on the autistic spectrum.

Both Caroline & Justin are national Triathlon England medallists (they rightly claim that National Club Relay Veteran - Silver and Bronze medals count) and have both won Triathlon England's 'East Midlands Children's Coach of the Year' awards. Caroline has also won the Triathlon England 'National Children's Coach of the Year' and 'Rutland Coach of the Year' awards. Ketton Panthers Triathlon Club has won the prestigious 'East Midlands Series' as well as several 'Rutland Active' Awards.

ALSO AVAILABLE FROM THE AUTHORS

"This book should be the go-to manual for young, aspiring triathletes and their parents. Jam packed with tips, tricks and advice for all levels of athlete, it's perfect for the newcomer, the slightly more established youngster wanting to research a bit more or the parent trying to figure out how to best support their child(ren)."

VICKY HOLLAND
OLYMPIC BRONZE MEDALLIST
AND ITU WORLD CHAMPION

Made in United States
North Haven, CT
10 July 2024

54548429R00043